JOHN PETER WILD

TEXTILES IN ARCHAEOLOGY

D1502137

SHIRE ARCHAEOLOGY

2

Cover photograph
A fragment of all-wool tapestry from Roman Egypt depicting a female theatre-mask set amid garlands. It probably once bordered a curtain or coverlet and dates to the third century AD.
(Courtesy of the Manchester Museum.)

British Library Cataloguing in Publication Data:
Wild, John Peter
Textiles in archaeology — (Shire archaeology; 56).
1. Archaeological sources. Textiles. Interpretation
I. Title
930.1'028'5
ISBN 0 85263 931 7

Published in 2003 by
SHIRE PUBLICATIONS LTD
Cromwell House, Church Street, Princes Risborough,
Buckinghamshire HP27 9AA, UK.
(Website: www.shirebooks.co.uk)

Series Editor: James Dyer.

Number 56 in the Shire Archaeology series.

ISBN 0 85263 931 7.

First published 1988; reprinted 2003.

Printed in Great Britain by
CIT Printing Services Ltd, Press Buildings,
Merlins Bridge, Haverfordwest, Pembrokeshire SA61 1XF.

Contents

List of illustrations

Preface

Textile finds from archaeological sites provide insights into many facets of early man's social and economic progress. To appreciate how and why they do so it is useful to have some understanding of how textiles were made, and this survey traces the route of textile production from the raw materials to the finished goods. At each stage textile finds usually help to answer the technical questions they pose. In this book I have deliberately concentrated on the finds from Britain and north-west Europe simply because the textile research field is vast and so much progress has been made of late. An air of mystery still clings to textiles in archaeological circles: I hope this book may help to dispel it.

Acknowledgements

Warmest thanks are due to Mrs F. C. Wild for reading and criticising the manuscript: blemishes that remain are my fault. The Classical Faculty of the University of Cambridge kindly allowed me to reproduce figures 21, 24, 28, 37 and 44 from my book *Textile Manufacture in the Northern Roman Provinces*. Miss P. Wild prepared figure 8.

Chronology in Britain

The dates below are not to be taken too literally. Prehistorians depend ultimately on radiocarbon dating. Traditional divisions between the later historical periods are somewhat arbitrary.

Neolithic	4000 BC	–	2500 BC
Early bronze age	2500 BC	–	1800 BC
Late bronze age	1800 BC	–	800 BC
Iron age	800 BC	–	AD 43
Roman period	AD 43	–	AD 410
Early (pagan) Anglo-Saxon period	AD 410	–	AD 650
Middle Saxon	AD 650	–	AD 850
Late Saxon	AD 850	–	AD 1066
Viking (Anglo-Scandinavian)	AD 850	–	AD 1066

1. Iron age costume from a northern European peat-bog: a woman's clothing from the Huldremose, Randers, Denmark. Her skirt and the scarf round her neck are of wool in 2/2 twill weave with a check pattern. The cape is of sheepskin. (Courtesy of the National Museum, Copenhagen.)

1
The survival of textiles

Even archaeologists, on being told of research in progress on textiles from archaeological sites, have asked 'Do any exist?' A few outstanding textiles with early historical associations, like the Bayeux Tapestry or the Turin Shroud, are famous, but they are not archaeological finds. In early societies woven fabrics served several extremely important functions, and the excavator could expect their remains to turn up as commonly as potsherds. They rarely do, however, except under special climatic conditions or in a microenvironment which allows normally perishable organic materials to survive.

Dry conditions

The dry, often salt-laden environment of the desert has minimal bacterial activity and is ideal for the preservation of textile fabrics of all sorts. Readers may be familiar with 'Coptic' textiles from Egypt displayed in many museums in Britain and abroad. Like the piece illustrated on the front cover, they are mostly fragments of brightly coloured tapestry-woven decoration which once enlivened the tunics, cloaks, curtains, cushions and bedspreads of the Roman and Islamic inhabitants of the Nile Valley. Original colours are intact. The ancient Egyptians preferred undyed, pleated linens and these, too, remain in pristine condition in the dry climate (see Rosalind Hall's *Egyptian Textiles*, Shire Egyptology 4). On some settlement sites in the Near East the excavator is faced with a problem unthinkable elsewhere: how to store or dispose of a great volume of rags, once they have been recorded.

Wet conditions

In northern and central Europe, by contrast, peat-bogs, lakes and stream-beds provide the principal insights into the work of early spinners and weavers. Here constant moisture, the exclusion of air and permeation by humic acids secure the preservation of organic materials.

In 1850 peat-diggers discovered the body of a man on Grewelthorpe Moor near Kirkby Malzeard in North Yorkshire, clad in a 'toga of a green colour while some portions of the dress were of a scarlet hue; the stockings were of yellow cloth'. Evidently this was a bog-burial; but, alas for scientific research, he was re-interred in the local churchyard, and only a shoe and parts of a stocking eventually reached the Yorkshire Museum in York; the shoe shows he was a Roman. Such glimpses of a complete costume are rare among the bog-finds in Britain. Denmark, however, boasts a vast collection of whole garments of prehistoric and early historic date (figure 1), mostly recovered from the lakes and bogs of the Jutland peninsula. Some of them were flung into the waters by iron age man as a gesture of dedication to the gods, while others had been worn by outcasts and miscreants condemned to solitary burial in the fen wastes.

Man-made moist environments also contribute to textile history. At Vindolanda (Chesterholm) near Hadrian's Wall the early Roman forts (AD 90-120) were built across a damp hollow in the ground, a natural dumping ground for rubbish that included several hundred woollen rags. In medieval towns like London, York, Newcastle, Perth and Dublin the lower occupation layers are beneath the water-table and have consequently preserved a great corpus of textile material – evidence not just for textile technology, but for clothing fashions too.

In the damp anaerobic conditions just described some textiles survive better than others, but the reasons for this are not fully understood. In general terms, while hair and wool (i.e. animal protein) fibres are well preserved, flax (a cellulosic plant fibre) is rarely found and, presumably, decayed rapidly. Most bogs are acidic, which would accelerate the decomposition of flax fibres; a few are alkaline and that in theory should have the reverse effect. Certainly the chalky sediment on the bed of some Swiss lakes has yielded a remarkable series of neolithic textiles, of flax and tree bast fibres.

Wool cloth found in damp places is usually a shade of 'peat brown' with occasional hints of other colours, some of which can be identified by dye analysis (see chapter 8). As it dries out, the cloth loses some of its flexibility, individual fibres break off, and the material requires gentle handling.

Replacement by metal salts

The metal corrosion products which encase objects of iron or copper alloy buried in the ground are an increasingly fruitful source of textile information. The main focus of interest is on burials (figure 2). In Anglo-Saxon cemeteries, for instance, the dead were laid to rest in their own clothes; for women that meant tunics pinned on each shoulder with a bronze brooch. If there were iron weapons or utensils furnishing men's graves, they too came into contact with the clothing as they rusted

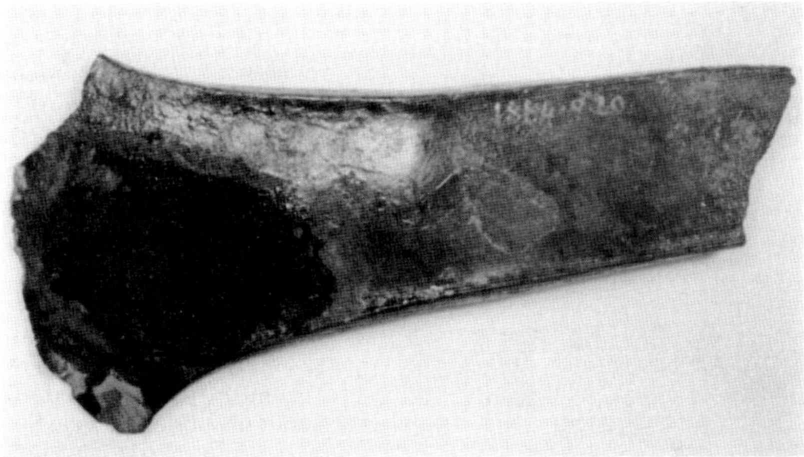

2. Patch of fine plain-weave linen (2 by 3.5 cm; ¾ inch by 1⅜ inches) preserved in the corrosion products of a bronze axe from Barrow 7 on the Dorset Ridgeway. Early bronze age. (Courtesy of Dorset Natural History and Archaeological Society, Dorset County Museum, Dorchester.)

3. Scanning electron microscope photograph of wool fibres preserved as a cast in an amalgam of iron corrosion products on a late sixth- or seventh-century spearhead from an Anglo-Saxon cemetery at Bargates, Dorset. (Courtesy of Robert Janaway, University of Bradford.)

4. Carbonised remains of a twill couch or mattress cover of wool from Colchester, Essex, still lying where it was destroyed by Boudica's followers in the uprising of AD 60-1. (Courtesy of Colchester Archaeological Trust.)

5. Negative impression of plain-weave cloth on a Roman tile from Hockwold-cum-Wilton, Norfolk. The cloth (perhaps a glove) was wrapping the tilemaker's knuckles as he stacked the unfired tiles (scale 3:2). (Courtesy of the Norfolk Archaeological Unit; photograph by David Wicks.)

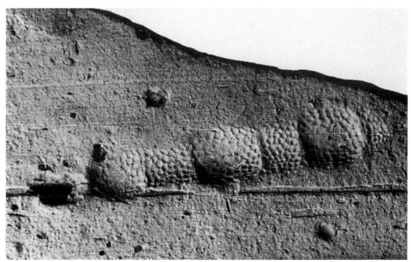

away (figure 3). Gradually the sulphides leaching out of the metal invaded the adjacent patches of textile, replacing the constituent animal or vegetable fibres or causing a negative cast to be formed around them. Little or nothing of the original cloth remains, but its outward form can be studied and some significant facts can be gleaned about the garments worn by the deceased.

Lead salts, too, have a preservative quality. A Roman lead coffin at St Albans was found to contain the remains of a child, its head supported on a wad of wool cloth which was still in fair condition owing to the ground moisture and sulphides exuded by the lead.

Some unusual cases

In AD 60 Boudica's rebel forces set fire to timber buildings inside the Roman legionary base at Colchester. A mattress lying in a corner of one of the rooms was not consumed by the heat, but carbonised (like the woodwork at Herculaneum). The diamond twill weave of its blackened wool cover (figure 4) could still be recognised, but under the microscope the fibres in its yarns were heavily distorted.

Workers making building tiles, pottery or even the clay vessels for refining salt sometimes handled their products inadvertently before they were properly dry. The result was a negative impression in the clay of the clothing covering a knee or elbow or protecting the hands (figure 5). The image is often crisp and clear, but in recording it allowance has to be made for some shrinkage in drying or firing. Impressions of a similar type have been noted in the late Roman gypsum burials from Dorchester, Dorset, and York. The body was laid out in layers of gypsum powder which solidified and still carry the marks of the wrapping round the corpse.

Gold thread does not decay. Among the Anglo-Saxon aristo-cracy garments trimmed with tablet-woven braids were popular and were sometimes enhanced with brocaded 'floating' gold weft. Even when the wool, silk or flax of the braid has disintegrated, the structure of the weave may still be reflected in undulations on the gold brocade.

Of perennial fascination for textile experts are the sealed tombs of prominent ecclesiastical figures of the middle ages. The microclimate inside the coffin may be sufficiently stable for some of the original vestments and furnishing to survive. The tomb of St Cuthbert in Durham Cathedral with its rich silks, embroideries and tablet-weaves has confirmed in spectacular fashion what the literary sources tell us of the skills of Anglo-Saxon weavers and needlewomen.

The size of a surviving textile fragment is no guide to its importance. Two minute pieces of silk, for instance, one from Holborough in Kent, the other from Colchester, Essex, have shed a completely new light on trading connections between Roman Britain, Roman Syria and Han China. A secure archaeological findspot, however, is crucial, for out of context ancient textiles rarely look ancient! Bits of modern denim, cotton bandage and jute sacking accidentally trodden by an excavator into the muddy layer on which he was working have been brought to the writer for examination. Some were rejected at once — others nearly reached the printed page.

6. A recent wool fibre showing overlapping scales (scale approximately 1:3000). (Scanning electron microscope photograph by courtesy of W. D. Cooke, UMIST.)

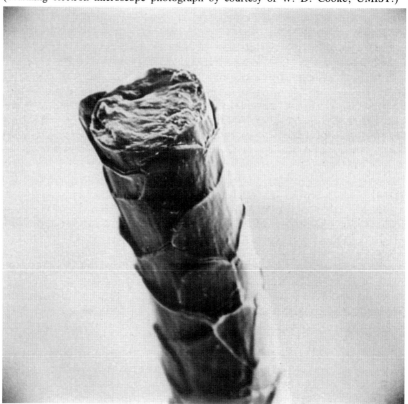

2
Fibres and their preparation

Early man had a surprisingly firm grasp of the mechanical properties of the various natural fibres which were available to him. Rope, basketry, matting, netting, woven fabrics and felt were all end-products of centuries of practical experiment. The domestication of plants and animals during the so-called neolithic revolution had introduced new sources of fibre, but the constraints of geography and climate limited their availability. Some experiments involved what we would call exotica: asbestos fibres, for instance, and the silky strands with which the *Pinna nobilis*, a giant Mediterranean mussel, anchors itself to the sea-bed. None the less, the potential of a select handful of the more familiar natural fibres was recognised at an early date and they played a dominant role in the European textile industry until the advent of modern synthetics.

The principal raw materials of ancient textiles in Europe were sheep's wool and flax while animal hair, hemp and other plant fibres had a subsidiary position. The leading imported fibres were silk and cotton, luxuries until at least early modern times. Preparation of the raw fibres for spinning was often time-consuming, labour-intensive and specialised, and each fibre category demanded appropriate treatment. In what follows the main fibres and their particular modes of preparation will be considered in turn.

Wool

The sheep was domesticated by about 8000 BC in north-east Iraq, and by 3000 BC at the latest there are firm indications that its coat was being converted into wool felt or woven fabric. In Britain the earliest finds of sheep bones date to the early neolithic (from about 4000 BC), but the first extant wool textiles are early bronze age, such as those from the oak coffin in a barrow at Rylston, East Yorkshire (about 2300 BC). That is no surprise, for analysis of the earliest textiles from Europe and western Asia has proved them all to be of plant origin until almost the end of the neolithic.

The wild sheep grew an outer layer of short hair-like kemps and a sparse undercoat of short-stapled fine wool. After domestication the woolly undercoat became denser, and many of the kemps in the outer coat were replaced by long-stapled wool.

7. An Orkney ram, breed champion at the Rare Breeds Survival Trust Show and Sale. (Photograph by S. R. F. Tupper.)

Eventually, probably as a result of direct selection by man, there evolved a uniform fleece of generalised medium wool.

We have gained our understanding of the evolution just described and of the improvements to the sheep's fleece in prehistoric times from studying the yarns in wool textiles from a representative and geographically widespread series of archaeological sites. Dr Michael Ryder, who pioneered the work, has shown that by measuring a sample of 100 wool fibres from a yarn and plotting the fibre diameter distribution as a histogram conclusions can be drawn about the character of the fleece from which the wool came. Much rests on the assumption that the yarn is truly representative of the fleece, and some misgivings have been expressed about this.

A wool fibre has a thick central cortex and a thinner cuticle or surface layer which consists of flat overlapping scales (figure 6). The outer edges of the scale project slightly and this helps the fibre to interlock with its neighbours to build a stable yarn or felt. Coarser wool fibres sometimes have a hollow central core (medulla) and in naturally coloured wools pigment granules can be identified. Kemp has similar characteristics to wool, but its central medulla is larger and normally collapsed; a kemp can be recognised by the pointed tip at each end.

The first sheep were dark brown with paler underbelly wool like their wild ancestor, but white was the dominant gene and as the early farmers began to breed selectively so white or grey animals became commoner. Analysis of prehistoric textiles has revealed that by the iron age fleeces of various colours and tones — dark-brown, red-brown, light-brown, grey and white — would be found in the same flock.

Two Scottish breeds of sheep illustrate the early stages of fleece development. The more primitive is the Soay, a feral breed that flourishes on the islands of St Kilda in the Outer Hebrides, their home since at least the Viking era. They have a slender frame, long legs and a long neck and are exceptionally agile. The rams and many of the ewes are horned; both have short tails and they stand about 55 cm (21½ inches) at the shoulder. About 75 per cent of the St Kilda flock have a dark-brown fleece, the rest being light-brown. Most animals have a white underbelly and rump patch. There are two types of fleece: one, a hairy medium coat with fine kemps, is similar to that of the first domesticated sheep; the other is woolly, and the kemps have narrowed to give a coat of generalised medium wool. Staple length is short (up to 6 cm; 2⅜ inches) and fleeces weigh less than 0.68 kg (1½ pounds).

The Soay can be regarded as the typical bronze age sheep. By the iron age a new fleece type had evolved containing a wider range of fibres and colours. It is exemplified in the Orkney sheep (figure 7) which by a curious ecological and historical accident live on the seashore of North Ronaldsay on a diet of seaweed! Grey fleeces (in fact a mixture of white and dark fibres) predominate, but there are also white or near-white, reddish-brown and dark-brown animals.

One cannot properly speak of 'breeds' in Britain until the late middle ages, but some broad distinctions can be made (figure 8). By the end of the Roman period what we technically call shortwool, longwool and medium-wool fleeces are attested, and comparison between the sizes of sheep longbones hints that some larger-bodied animals could be seen by then. The influence of Viking settlers may be behind the black-faced horned hairy sheep of central and north-eastern Britain, but while we can chart from documentary evidence the rise of the historic English woollen industry and speak with confidence on monastic flock management, there is still a lack of data on contemporary fleece and body conformation.

8. The changing outward forms of the sheep: (above) a Soay ram from Lieutenant-General Pitt-Rivers's flock; (centre) a fifteenth-century polled ewe (after Armitage); (below) a New Leicester wether (castrated male) of about 1835 (after Shiels).

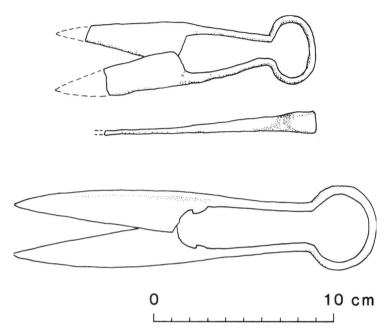

9. (Above) Roman sheep shears of iron from Barton Court Farm, Oxfordshire (after Miles); (below) thirteenth-century shears from Fyfield, Wiltshire (after Fowler).

Like other wild creatures, the primitive sheep moulted in spring or early summer, and after domestication it continued to shed its fleece, aided by man. Plucking was the normal method of retrieving wool until the invention of shears in the iron age, and Shetlanders are still 'rooing' their flocks today. Plucking has the advantage over shearing of taking mainly the finer wool fibres (the kemps do not fall out until the autumn), but inevitably there is considerable wool loss in the opening stages of the moult. Shearing secures the whole fleece, and yarns spun from shorn wool are therefore a more reliable guide to fleece type. Sheep which are regularly shorn lose the tendency to moult and develop a continuously growing coat which cannot then be plucked.

Sheep shears have a traditional form which has changed remarkably little over 2500 years (figure 9). A pair of tapering confronted blades is linked by a bow-shaped spring which parts the cutting edges after each stroke. Shears were used for a multitude of purposes, and the function of an individual pair can

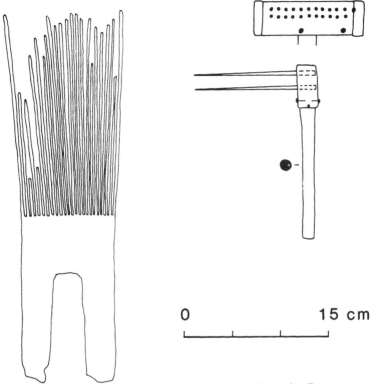

0   15 cm

10. (Left) Flat iron woolcomb of East Anglian type from the Roman town of Caistor-by-Norwich, Norfolk; (right) restored drawing of a Norwegian Viking woolcomb with wooden handle, two rows of pointed iron teeth and a wooden head cased in metal sheet.

rarely be deduced from its archaeological findspot but for sheep shearing a blade length of 10 to 15 cm (4 to 6 inches) may be the optimum.

Wool can be spun directly from the fleece, but spinning is made easier by preliminary manual and mechanical sorting. Perhaps as early as the Roman period, the medieval and modern distinction may have been drawn between finer combed worsted yarns (containing mainly long-stapled fibres) and the heavier woollen yarns (of mostly short staples). The earliest unequivocal worsted yarns in Britain have been recognised in textiles from Anglo-Scandinavian York and late Saxon London; but finds of Roman woolcombs in southern and eastern England suggest that the Romans, too, combed some of their wool to separate long from short fibres.

Roman woolcombs are flat iron plates up to 35 cm (13¾ inches) long with teeth cut or welded into one or both ends (figure 10). In operation they were fixed into combing posts and the wool mass was drawn repeatedly through the teeth. Wool-combing was only slowly mechanised after the industrial revolution, and professional hand-woolcombers were still at work in the Pennines in the nineteenth century. Their combs, used in pairs, consisted of several rows of pointed iron teeth anchored into a T-shaped wooden bar with projecting handle. Almost exactly the same type was already in use in seventh-century Saxon England and at a slightly later date they are found in Viking women's graves.

We are familiar today with hand-cards, wooden boards set with tiny metal hooks on which wool fibres can be teased out before spinning. The first evidence for such implements dates to the fourteenth century.

Fibres of animals other than sheep are rare on north European archaeological sites. One may quote goat-hair cloth from early medieval London, horse (tail) hair in the gold threads of the late Saxon embroideries at Maaseik (Belgium) and horse hair in the magnificent late bronze age tasselled belt from Armoy, County Antrim (figure 11).

11. Horse-hair tasselled belt found in a peat-bog at Armoy, County Antrim, with late bronze age metalwork. It is 4.6 cm (about 1¾ inches) wide. (Courtesy of the National Museum of Ireland, Dublin.)

12. Flax fibres in a heavily worn modern linen sheet. Nodes are visible as striations across the fibres (scale approximately 1:425). (Scanning electron microscope photograph by courtesy of W. D. Cooke, UMIST.)

13. Bast fibre string from the neolithic causewayed site at Etton, Peterborough. (Courtesy of the Trustees of the British Museum and Fenland Archaeological Trust.)

Flax, hemp, nettle

Growing, harvesting and preparing plant fibres for textile purposes is particularly laborious, but bast fibres from the stem of a plant or tree were the first materials to be spun by man and converted into woven fabrics (figure 12). The neolithic linen textiles from Catal Hüyük in Anatolia (about 6000 BC) are the earliest attested cloth remains, but several other finds from the Near East are not much later in date. The best known group of early European linens are from the neolithic lakeside villages of Switzerland (3200-2600 BC). No neolithic fabrics have yet been uncovered in Britain; but a length of string (figure 13) from the neolithic causewayed site at Etton, Peterborough, made from an unidentified bast fibre (perhaps lime), indicates the potential.

Flax *(Linum usitatissimum)* is the principal European plant fibre (figure 14). The fibres themselves grow between the outer bark of the stem and its woody core. Under the microscope they have diagnostic nodes or knots at intervals (like bamboo) and a hollow centre.

Flax seed is sown in March or April in northern Europe, on well drained fertile soils. The mature plants stand up to 1 metre (3

14. (Left) Flax plant carrying ripened seeds (scale 1:14); (right) head of flax in bloom; (below) a seed capsule (both just over life size).

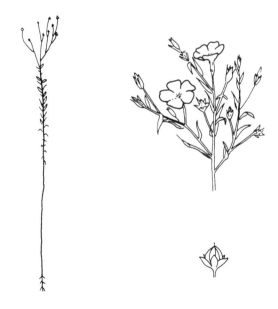

feet 3 inches) high, crowned by tiny white or blue flowers. They ripen five to six months after sowing but are harvested before the seeds are fully ripe, i.e. before the woody core hardens, if they are to be used for textiles rather than linseed. The stalks were pulled by hand in antiquity for maximum length and the seed bolls removed by combing. Then began the tedious business of separating the usable fibre from the rest of the cellulosic plant mass. First the stems were submerged in stagnant water for two to three weeks ('retting') so that bacteria loosened the fibres from the core and bark. Then they were thoroughly dried and beaten with a wooden mallet on a flat surface ('breaking'). 'Scutching' followed, in which the stems were struck with a heavy wooden blade over a narrow edge to release the bark. Finally the fibres were combed through a flax hackle, a board set with several rows of vertical iron spikes, to dispose of any remaining woody particles. Traditional – and effective – methods like these have been followed for at least two millennia.

While there is no lack of linen textiles from later prehistoric, Roman and Anglo-Saxon Britain, our knowledge of contemporary flax raising and its economics is thin. Even finds of seeds could point to cultivation for linseed, not fibre. In medieval and modern times the flax fields of northern France, the Low Countries and the Baltic states dominated the market, and flax grown in the British Isles was not competitive.

Hemp *(Cannabis sativa)* is a taller and hardier plant than flax, and its coarser fibres are more suited to ropemaking and heavy-duty sail- and sack-cloth than clothing fabrics. Cultivation, harvesting and extraction are as for flax, and individual fibres are hard to distinguish from those of linen under the microscope. The first satisfactory record of hemp in Britain is seeds from a Roman well in York, and a pollen curve from East Anglia indicates its cultivation there throughout the Anglo-Saxon period.

Nettlecloth made from the common stinging nettle *(Urtica dioica)* sounds an unlikely fashion fabric, but it was vastly popular in the late eighteenth century in Scandinavia. That was a revival, for the first known find of nettlecloth dates to the late bronze age (Voldtofte in Denmark); possible finds from Britain are not confirmed. The fibres, white, silky and up to 50 mm (2 inches) long, are extracted by retting, breaking, scutching and hackling.

All the fibres described so far have been the product of farming in temperate Europe. Two more, silk and cotton, are not native to the region, but played and still play a prominent part in our clothing and textile trade.

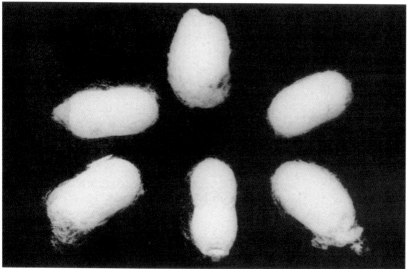

15. Modern cocoons of the cultivated silk moth *Bombyx mori* (scale about 2:3)

Silk

China is the home of the mulberry silk moth *(Bombyx mori)*, the larva of which, the 'silkworm', spins the fibre. The caterpillar feeds ravenously on the leaves of the white or black mulberry and, when ready to pupate, envelops itself in a cocoon (figure 15) of silk fibre which issues as a double filament (a 'bave' comprising two 'brins') from glands on its lower lip. The cocoons are dropped into boiling water to kill the grubs and soften the sericin gum, and the filament is reeled off in unbroken lengths of up to 1000 metres (3300 feet). By contrast, the related wild silk moths of Asia spin shorter lengths which usually have to be given some twist like ordinary textile fibres.

Sericulture had begun in China in the third millennium BC and silk clothing became an important status symbol. By the first century AD silk fabrics were being imported from China into the Roman Empire over the long-distance land and sea routes in increasing quantity. In Britain the first attested find, a damask from Holborough in Kent, is late Roman. Of similar date is a piece of plain tabby silk from Colchester. Later the Anglo-Saxons used silk thread in tablet weaving and embroidery, and by the ninth century bonnets of silk imported from Byzantine or Arab silk-weaving centres were being worn in York, Lincoln, London and Dublin. By that date silkworms were being reared in the Mediterranean world and supplies could be secured from lands under Byzantine or Arab rule.

Cotton

The first cotton probably reached western Europe on the back of a traveller from Rome's eastern provinces. The Greeks and Romans knew it as a crop in the Nile Valley, parts of the Near East and India — but what species it was, tree or herbaceous cotton, is disputed.

Cotton fibres grow on the seeds within the plant's seed boll. When the plant ripens and the boll opens, seeds and fibre are plucked out by hand and then have to be separated from each other either by hand or (later) between the rollers of a gin. The fibres are short (up to 25 mm; 1 inch) and under the microscope resemble twisted ribbons.

The growth of interest in cotton fabrics in Europe stems from the westward expansion of the Arabs in the seventh century. Fustian, a cloth with cotton weft on linen warp, led the market in the earlier middle ages, first in Moorish Spain and later in Italy. It was not until the seventeenth century that the first major cotton spinning and weaving centres sprang up in England.

Anglo-Saxon ladies, but wooden ones must have been commoner. The pin-beater, a cigar-shaped bone implement pointed at both ends, is another Anglo-Saxon weaver's aid to releasing knots and tangles.There was a simpler version in iron age Britain. More controversial are the long-handled bone or antler combs from iron age and sometimes Roman sites; they have been identified as weaving combs, but with their short stubby teeth and curved cross-section they are not ideal for pushing through the warp to beat up the weft (figure 23).

The woollen rugs woven today on the Norwegian warp-weighted loom have a distinctive feature, a starting border, which occurs in almost identical form on many of the earliest textiles in prehistoric Europe. The starting border's prime function is to secure the main warp to the cloth-beam on the warp-weighted loom. It is woven beforehand on a small band loom (using rigid heddle or tablets, see below). In preparing a starting border (figure 24) the weaver draws through the open shed of the band warp (A) a loop of yarn (C) from the ball of the weft (B) on the left-hand side. The loop is pulled far to the right and slipped

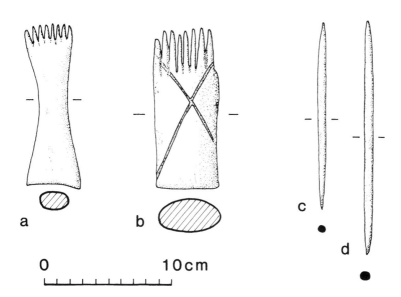

23. Bone tools for beating up the weft: (a, b) late iron age combs from the Broch of Burrian, Orkney (after MacGregor); (c) Anglo-Saxon pin-beater from Sutton Courtenay, Oxfordshire (after Leeds); (d) middle Saxon pin-beater from Castor, Peterborough.

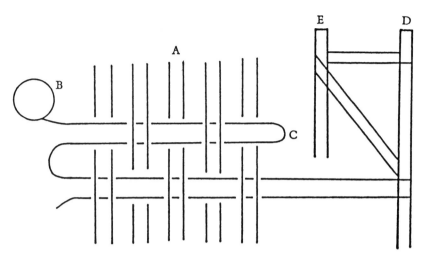

24. Weaving a starting border; (A) warp of band; (B) ball of weft yarn; (C) loop pulled with finger through band's shed; (D and E) pegs round or over which the loop of weft is passed.

round and over two pegs (E and D). When the band is complete, the loops formed round peg D are cut — and, if the warping has been done consistently, the cutting will divide the warp automatically into a bundle of odd-numbered and a bundle of even-numbered threads, ready to be tied to the back and front rows of loomweights. Finds of loomweights and sometimes of woven starting borders on textiles make us confident that the warp-weighted loom was the standard equipment of the weaver in Britain from the bronze age until perhaps the twelfth century AD.

Two-beam loom

A second type of vertical loom is attested in ancient Europe, one on which the weights have been replaced by another horizontal beam linking the uprights (figure 25). It is shown in ancient Egyptian and Roman art and mentioned in classical literature. There is circumstantial evidence for it, too, in iron age Denmark, but there is no living European tradition of its use today. Scandinavians call it the 'tubular loom'; for, if the warp spanned between the two beams reverses over a horizontal stick at the front, then, after the weaving is complete and the stick replaced by a cord, the resulting textile is a tube. Remove the cord, and the cloth can be laid flat as a cloak or blanket. Every Anglo-Saxon site has its loomweights, but in Roman Britain they are curiously rare. Perhaps the two-beam loom from the Mediterranean was competing successfully, if briefly, with the warp-weighted loom at that time.

Horizontal loom

The thirteenth century AD, it has been claimed, was an era of textile revolution, and certainly by that date a new loom had emerged on the European industrial scene, a sturdy handloom with horizontally spanned warp (figure 26). It was fitted with harnesses (upgraded versions of the heddle-rods) linked over pulleys to treadles for opening the sheds, a built-in reed for beating up the weft and a boat-shaped shuttle for carrying the weft-spool – all quite new.

The origin of the European handloom is much debated. It is probably not descended from the loom of Rome's eastern provinces on which damask silk and fancy compound cloth was

25. Weaving on a reconstructed vertical two-beam loom at the Historical-Archaeological Research Centre, Lejre, Denmark. The loom is set up for weaving 2/2 twill with three heddle-rods and (above) a shed-rod. (Photograph by Ole Malling.)

26. A medieval horizontal loom illustrated in a manuscript of about 1250 in Trinity College, Cambridge. It is fitted with treadles (worked by the weaver's feet) which are bound over pulleys to a pair of shafts opening the shed. The weaver grasps a boat-shuttle in his right hand and beats up the weft with a reed controlled by his left hand.

woven; for this was probably vertical, though equipped with multiple heddle-rods or other complex pattern-making devices. Ultimately this advanced loom became horizontal, but we do not know when. The earliest handloom was a more workaday tool.

Large webs of cloth up to 3 metres (9 feet 10 inches) wide – indeed most commonly whole garments – were woven on the two simpler types of vertical loom. The medieval handloom, however, while narrower, had a much longer warp suited to producing bolts of cloth which was the currency of the medieval textile trade and the basic stuff of the tailor.

Small looms

Many sorts of smaller loom were current in antiquity for weaving narrow fabrics – girdles, leggings, decorative braids and starting borders. We can say little about them, for if their warp were stretched between the weaver's belt and a tree or a table-leg there would be no archaeological trace.

We can recognise two devices for opening the shed on a narrow warp: the rigid heddle (figure 27) and weaving tablets. The rigid heddle of bone or wood was a flat frame with alternating slots and slats with holes through which the warp threads passed. By raising or depressing the heddle, two different sheds could be

27. Part of a Roman rigid heddle from South Shields, Tyne and Wear. It is of bone, encased top and bottom in sheet bronze binding. (Courtesy of the University of Newcastle Museum of Antiquities and Society of Antiquaries of Newcastle upon Tyne.)

opened, the one above, the other below the general level of the warp. The first datable rigid heddle is Roman, from South Shields, Tyne and Wear.

Tablet weaving, which has experienced a modest craft revival in modern times, is one of the oldest European textile techniques, traceable at least to the early iron age. The tablets are small flat squares (sometimes triangles) of bone or wood with a hole in each corner through which a warp-thread is passed. When set up, the tablets are held in the hand like a pack of cards, parallel to the warp, and turned back or forward by half or quarter turns (figure 28). This action twists the four (or three) warp-threads controlled by each tablet into a cord that can be locked into position by weft thread inserted between the turns and remaining invisible. By varying the colours of the warp yarn and the direction of turn of the tablets, intricate warp patterns can be executed. The Anglo-Saxons and Vikings wove some beautiful braids on tablets, enhanced by floating (brocaded) gold thread; more prosaically, selvedges on cloaks were strengthened by integrated tablet-woven borders.

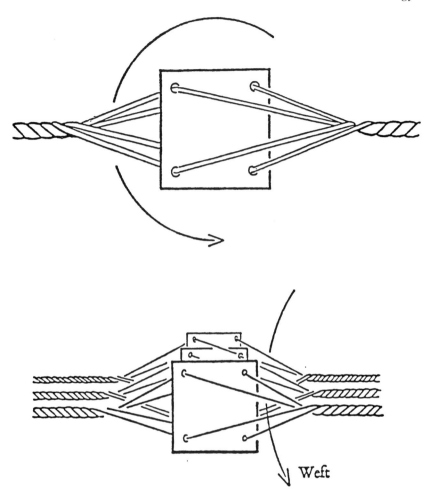

28. Tablet weaving: (above) how a single four-hole tablet is threaded up and turned; (below) how a pack of tablets is manipulated and the weft inserted between the threads passing through the two upper and two lower holes.

Weaves

Thanks to some discoveries of comparatively large bodies of material from individual archaeological sites, it is becoming possible to classify textiles by quality, that is, not by a single criterion (such as weave structure), but by fibre, yarn, weave and finish assessed together. But for most finds weave remains the simplest means of characterisation.

In *plain* or *tabby weave* (figures 29, 30) the weft passes under and over successive single warp-threads – the process described above on the warp-weighted loom. Tabby is *de rigueur* for linen in virtually every age and region, and also for most bronze age woollen cloth. If the warp and weft are paired, it is called *basket weave;* if just warp or weft is paired, it is *half-basket weave.*

At the end of the bronze age the first *two-over-two twill* appeared, a distinctive diagonal weave in which the passage of successive weft-threads is staggered by one warp-thread to right or left. To weave it on the warp-weighted loom, four separate sheds had to be opened, probably by means of three heddle-rods and a movable shed-rod. Once the value of twill for creating stable fabrics was appreciated (primarily in wool, though the Anglo-Saxons, curiously, used it for linens, too), it became increasingly popular. Towards the close of the pre-Roman iron age two more complicated variants appeared, *herringbone*

29. Silk ribbon in plain tabby weave from Milk Street, London. Maximum width is 1.2 cm (⁷/₁₆ inch). Late ninth or early tenth century. (Courtesy of the Museum of London; photograph by J. Bailey.)

Textiles in Archaeology

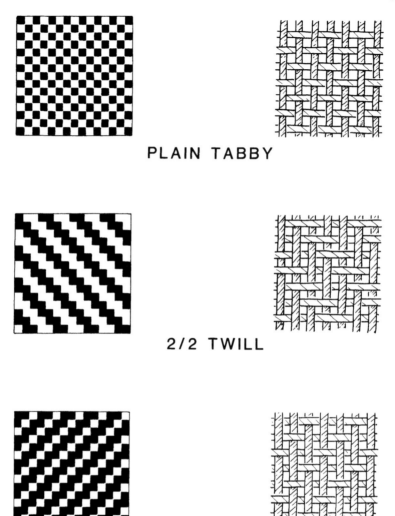

PLAIN TABBY

2/2 TWILL

2/1 TWILL

30. Conventional weaving drafts (left) and corresponding schematised drawings (right) of plain tabby weave, simple 2/2 twill and simple 2/1 twill. Black squares in the drafts show where the warp-threads, running vertically, pass over weft-threads. The drawings are twice the size of the drafts.

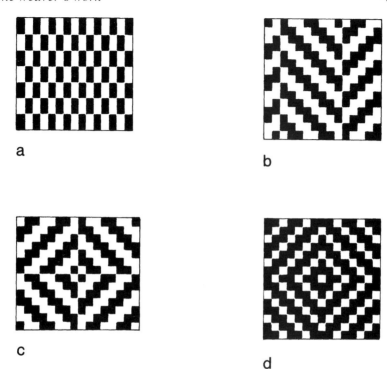

a

b

c

d

31. Drafts of variations of the principal weaves: (a) half-basket weave; (b) herringbone (warp-chevron) 2/2 twill; (c) diamond 2/2 twill; (d) diamond 2/1 twill. Black squares denote where the warp-threads pass over the weft-threads.

(warp-chevron) twill and *diamond twill* (figures 31 and 32). Before long diamond twill was taken up by weavers throughout northern Europe and it stayed pre-eminent there for the next millennium.

A second twill structure, *two-over-one twill,* emerged in the north in the first century AD, but it remained of minor significance, regarded perhaps as a simple pattern-weave. (If warp and weft are in contrasting colours, each colour dominates one face of the cloth, i.e. it is reversible.) Roman and Anglo-Saxon 2/1 twills tend to be quite fine, if rare; but the Vikings, if not the Saxons, introduced a new fashion for 2/1 diamond (lozenge) twill which became the principal luxury product of English weavers in the twelfth and thirteenth centuries (figure 33). Both types of twill (2/1 and 2/2) could be woven (it is thought) on both types of vertical loom, but there has been some

32. Fragment of 2/2 diamond twill in wool from Milk Street, London. The centres of the diamonds are 1.2 cm (⁷⁄₁₆ inch) apart horizontally. Late ninth century. (Courtesy of the Museum of London; photograph by J. Bailey.)
33. Length of fine 2/1 diamond twill from Lloyds Bank, Pavement, York. The centres of the diamonds are 2.3 cm (¹³⁄₁₆ inch) apart horizontally. Viking. (Courtesy of the York Archaeological Trust; photograph by M. S. Duffy.)

Hoo, however, could well have been an import. In an exciting series of developments in the silk weavers' workshops of the Roman Empire, an advanced vertical loom was built to produce mechanically patterned cloth – damask silk (figure 37), weft-faced compound tabby silks and woollens, and by AD 500 weft-faced compound twills. Such exotica reached the north as imports, to late Saxon London, for example, and to towns throughout the Viking world. Diplomatic channels brought westward some splendid Byzantine silks, but they survive today more often in church treasuries than on humble archaeological sites.

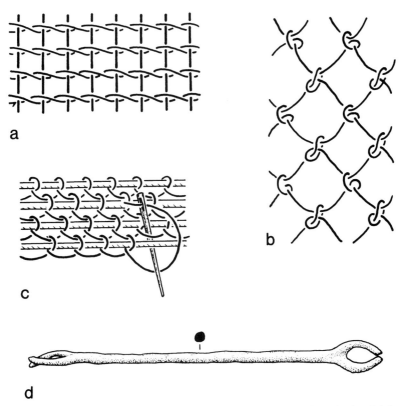

38. Basketry and netting structures and a netting needle: (a) basketry with twined weft (after Vogt); (b) the 'Lake Dwelling knot' in netting from neolithic Switzerland (after Vogt); (c) looped needle-netting (*nålebinding*) over extra weft threads (after Bender Jørgensen); (d) a Roman bronze netting needle from Richborough, Kent (scale 2:3; after Bushe-Fox).

5
Non-woven fabrics

Non-woven fabrics are constructed of interlocked yarns (netting, knitting, plaiting) or interlocked fibres (felt) and they are probably prehistoric man's earliest forays into textile production. Woven cloth, with warp distinguished from weft, represents a step towards mechanisation.

Basketry, netting, matting and woven textiles are found in close association on neolithic sites in the Near East and Europe, but the differences between them are not clear-cut. Woven structures, for instance, based on pairs of 'weft-threads' twined round one another and imprisoning the 'warp-threads' are characteristic of neolithic basketry from the Swiss lakes and the Iberian peninsula (figure 38).

The dividing line between netting and knitting is equally elusive. Netting has a single thread system, each yarn being knotted at regular intervals round its neighbour to make an openwork mesh. Netting was used by neolithic fishermen and worn as clothing in Old Kingdom Egypt (2613-2181 BC).

To carry yarn in a way in which it can easily be passed through a loop, the so-called netting needle was invented. It has two prongs or forks, one at each end of a short shaft, and the yarn is wound longitudinally between them (figure 38d). Iron and bronze examples are known in Roman and post-Roman Europe, but most were probably of wood or bone. They could also be used for weaving any kind of narrow fabric.

Arguably the most sophisticated type of netting is 'sprang' – a technique of special renown in Scandinavia, where it first appears in the early bronze age (about 2000 BC). A favourite for hairnets, sprang crops up throughout the Old World and the New. Little has yet been found in Britain, but several museums have examples in heavy wool from Coptic Egypt.

To build sprang the yarn is spanned between two bars set in a frame (shown sometimes in Greek vase-paintings). Working from right to left, midway between the bars, the weaver plaits adjacent threads round one another (figure 39) and locks the plait by inserting two flat battens or rods into the shed and pushing them to top and bottom. The procedure is repeated with two more rods, and two areas of fabric are formed, structurally mirror images of one another, one above and one below. The final lock has to be sewn into position to prevent the whole creation from unravelling.

Knitting with two needles is a familiar domestic art today, but surprisingly it is not attested in England until the fifteenth century. It may have travelled westwards with the Arabs: supposed Roman examples are dubious. Instead, looped needle-netting (for which we borrow the Danish term *nålebinding*) is often used for flexible three-dimensional fabrics. The earliest north European find is from Tybrind Vig in Denmark and dates to the late mesolithic (about 4200 BC); this particular piece is reinforced with an extra thread system round which the loops are laid, presumably with a needle (figure 38). In late and post-Roman times the *nålebinding* technique was applied to mittens and socks – like the famous Viking sock from Coppergate, York (figure 40)

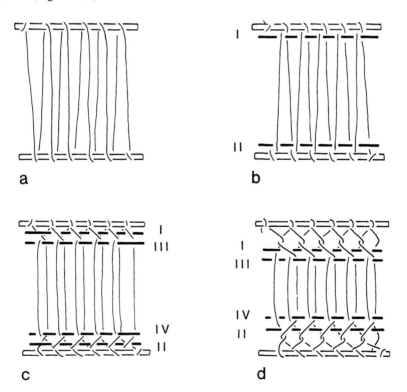

39. Plaiting simple sprang between two bars on a small loom: (a) warp set up; (b) rear warp brought forward and held by rods I and II; (c) rods III and IV inserted to hold the first cross in the warp top and bottom; (d) the position of the rods after two further moves, showing the first full plait.

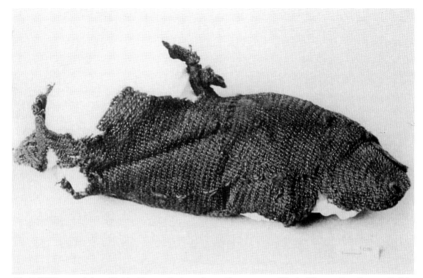

40. A Viking sock in *nålebinding* technique from Coppergate, York. The sockmaker probably used a bone needle and, beginning at the toe, built up systematically a series of rows of loops in plied wool yarn. (Courtesy of the York Archaeological Trust; photograph by M. S. Duffy.)

Finger plaiting of decorative cords and narrow braids is another prehistoric craft with a long history. The most attractive braids are Anglo-Saxon and later medieval, designed for attachment to garments.

Felt has played a lesser role in European cultural history than in that of western and central Asia. In Europe it has been used primarily as lining material, but the Romans shaped it into felt hats and contemplated using it for body armour. It is usually made from sheep's wool and exploits to the full the tendency of wool fibre scales to interlock when moisture and friction are applied. The first stage of felt-making is to lay the wool mass out in a thick layer and moisten it with warm water to promote shrinkage and movement. Then the mass is compressed by being rolled up in a carpet and rolled to and fro underfoot. The result is a resilient flexible sheet.

and heather, the former perhaps a mordant, the latter a dye-source. Yellow dyes are probably under-represented in the north European record because their spectra are masked by residual dirt from the samples. But weld *(Reseda luteola)* gives a sound yellow mordant-dye and is a native north European plant. Its seeds have been discovered in quantity at Dyer's Lane, Beverley, East Yorkshire, and in Bristol. Dyer's greenweed *(Genista tinctoria)* gives a yellow which can be dyed over woad to give green and is among the botanical remains from Coppergate and Bristol. Bog myrtle *(Myrica gale)*, found at Beverley, is another source of yellow.

Northern Europe was less obsessed than Rome or Byzantium with the meaning and chemistry of purple. 'True purple' was produced by a chain of specialised dyeworks around the east Mediterranean coast which relied on the dye fluid secreted by two whelks, *Murex brandaris* and *Murex trunculus* (figure 45). Their special colour constituent is 6,6'-dibromoindigotin, but the processes of extracting the dye and fixing it upon the fibres in the hot vat called for skill and great labour and are too complex to summarise here. The final chemical reaction in air could be halted when the right shade of 'purple' had been reached. So far only one instance of murex purple has been substantiated in Britain, in a Roman context. (A native British whelk, *Purpura lapillus*, also contains some dibromoindigotin.) Most ancient 'purples', however, turn out to be woad overdyed with madder, and much cheaper.

Insect dyes, though important in the Mediterranean in Roman times and earlier, made no impact on northern Europe until the middle ages. The kermes *(Kermococcus vermilio)*, an insect which infests the southern European kermes oak, yields a bright red dyestuff (kermesic acid) when crushed. It was being imported into Britain by the fifteenth century. Polish cochineal *(Porphyrophora polonica)*, a central European insect with similar properties, was also exploited in the middle ages, but the cochineal bug proper *(Dactylopius coccus)* was not known until after the discovery of America.

Structural evidence for dyeworks in the north is still meagre, considering that the vats must have been of durable materials. Foundations of heated vats have been uncovered in two twelfth-century houses in Winchester, and in Trig Lane, London, thirty such features of the same date have been excavated.

62

9
Glossary

Most technical terms used in this book are explained in the text or
illustrated. To check the meaning of a specific word the reader
should consult the index on page 67 and locate the relevant
passage. The entries below gloss terms which are either not
explained in the text or commonly cause confusion.

Boat-shuttle: a hollow wooden container shaped like a boat which
encapsulates a spool ('pirn') on which the weft yarn is wound.
Brocade: (verb) to add extra decorative threads during the
weaving process. Brocaded threads 'float' over parts of the
ground weave.
Nap: fibres which are drawn up from the surface of wool cloth to
make it feel soft like a blanket.
Pile: areas of projecting tufts or loops of yarn which are inserted
as extra threads during weaving parallel to the warp or weft of
the ground weave.
Reed: a comb-like implement with teeth set in a frame which is
attached by a horizontal pivot to the superstructure of a
horizontal loom. The reed is swung forward to beat up the weft
and its teeth maintain correct spacing across the warp.
Warp: the main system of threads on the loom. Warp runs
vertically on the warp-weighted and two-beam looms and is
shown running vertically in textile drafts and diagrams.
Weft: the system of threads introduced from the side by the
weaver to interlace with the warp. Weft runs *horizontally* on
the warp-weighted and two-beam looms and is shown horizontal in drafts and diagrams.

For a comprehensive account of textile terminology see
Burnham, D. K., *Warp and Weft,* Royal Ontario Museum,
Toronto, 1980. Not all the terms listed are current in Britain,
however.

10
Museums to visit

Great Britain

The British Museum, Great Russell Street, London WC1B 3DG. Telephone: 020 7323 8000 (switchboard), 020 7323 8299 (information desk). Website: www.thebritishmuseum.ac.uk Archaeological textiles and textile implements are displayed in several departments.

Butser Ancient Farm, Nexus House, Gravel Hill, Waterlooville, Hampshire PO8 0QE. Telephone: 023 9259 8838. Website: www.butser.org.uk Experimental iron age farm with rare breeds of sheep.

Cotswold Farm Park, Guiting Power, Cheltenham, Gloucestershire GL54 5UG. Telephone: 01451 850307. Website: www.cotswoldfarmpark.co.uk Early sheep breeds.

Jorvik Viking Centre, Coppergate, York YO1 9WT. Telephone: 01904 543403. Website: www.jorvik-viking-centre.co.uk Fascinating reconstructions of Viking crafts.

Lullingstone Silk Farm, Worldwide Butterflies, Compton House, Sherborne, Dorset DT9 4QN. Telephone: 01935 474608. First-hand introduction to the history of silk.

Petrie Museum of Egyptian Archaeology, University College London, Malet Place, London WC1E 6BT. Telephone: 020 7679 2884. Website: www.petrie.ucl.ac.uk Dynastic Egyptian and Coptic textiles.

Victoria and Albert Museum, Cromwell Road, South Kensington, London SW7 2RL. Telephone: 020 7942 2000. Website: www.vam.ac.uk Coptic and Byzantine textile collections.

Vindolanda Museum, Bardon Mill, Hexham, Northumberland NE47 7JN. Telephone: 01434 344277. Website: www.vindolanda.com Roman textiles from Vindolanda fort.

Weald and Downland Open Air Museum, Singleton, Chichester, West Sussex PO18 0EU. Telephone: 01243 811363. Website: www.wealddown.co.uk Weaving and dyeing displays.

Whitworth Art Gallery, University of Manchester, Oxford Road, Manchester M15 6ER. Telephone: 0161 275 7450. Website: www.whitworth.man.ac.uk. Important collection of Coptic textiles.

Belgium

National Flax Museum, Doorniksesteenweg 228, Kortrijk. Displays on flax growing

Denmark

Historical-Archaeological Research Centre, Slangealleen 2, DK-4320 Lejre. Telephone: 0045 4648 0878. Website: www.lejre-center.dk Reconstructions of early farming and crafts including textiles.

National Museum of Denmark, Frederiksholms Kanal 12, DK 1220 Copenhagen K. Telephone: 0045 3313 4411. Website: www.natmus.dk An unrivalled collection of prehistoric textiles.

Germany

Schleswig-Holstein Museum of Prehistory and Early History, Schloss Gottorf, 2380 Schleswig. Iron age costumes from the Jutland peninsula.

11
Further reading

Information on textiles from European archaeological sites tends to be published in learned journals that are not easily accessible to the general reader. Moreover, the most exciting results of the latest research at any given time will not be immediately available in print. None the less, the literature cited below should point the reader in the right direction and help him or her to explore the field.

General
Barber, E. J. W. *Prehistoric Textiles.* Princeton University Press, 1991. Comprehensive review of prehistoric textiles in the Near East and Europe.
Bender Jørgensen, L. *North European Textiles until AD 1000.* Aarhus University Press, 1992. Essential databank and discussion of archaeological textiles in Britain, Germany and Scandinavia.
Jenkins, D. J. *The Cambridge History of Western Textiles.* Cambridge University Press, 2003. The concise standard textbook.
Seiler-Baldinger, A. *Textiles: A Classification of Techniques.* Crawford House Press, 1994.
Walton Rogers, P.; Bender Jørgensen, L.; and Rast-Eicher, A. *The Roman Textile Industry and Its Influence.* Oxbow Books, 2001.

British textiles
Crowfoot, E. C. 'The Textiles' in *The Sutton Hoo Ship Burial,* edited by R. Bruce-Mitford, volume 3, I, 409-79. British Museum Press, 1983.
Crowfoot, E. C.; Pritchard, F.; and Staniland, K. *Textiles and Clothing c.1150–c.1450.* HMSO, 1992.
Henshall, A. S. 'Textiles and Weaving Appliances in Prehistoric Britain', *Proceedings of the Prehistoric Society,* volume 16 (new series, 1950), 130-62.
Walton, P. 'The Textiles' in Harbottle, B., and Ellison, M. 'An Excavation in the Castle Ditch, Newcastle upon Tyne, 1974–6', *Archaeologia Aeliana,* volume 9 (fifth series, 1981), 190-228.
Walton, P. 'Textiles, Cordage and Raw Fibre from 16-22 Coppergate', *The Archaeology of York,* volume 17, number 5. York Archaeological Trust, 1989.
Walton Rogers, P. 'Textile Production at 16-22 Coppergate', *The Archaeology of York,* volume 17, number 11. York Archaeological Trust, 1997.

Wild, J. P. *Textile Manufacture in the Northern Roman Provinces.* Cambridge University Press, 1970.
Wild, J. P. 'The Textile Industries of Roman Britain', *Britannia*, volume 33 (2002), 1-42.

Coptic textiles
De Moor, A. *Coptic Textiles from Flemish Private Collections.* Provincial Archaeological Museum of South-east Flanders, 1993. Specially good on dyes and technology.
Thompson, D. *Coptic Textiles in the Brooklyn Museum.* Brooklyn Museum, 1971. Old, but good starting point.

North European textiles
Hald, M. *Ancient Danish Textiles from Bogs and Burials.* National Museum of Denmark, 1980. A classic and fundamental report.
Schlabow, K. *Textilfunde der Eisenzeit in Nord-Deutschland.* Wachholtz, 1976. Outstanding artwork.

Technical topics
Balfour-Paul, J. *Indigo.* British Museum Press, 1998.
Birkett, M. E. *The Art of the Felt Maker.* Abbot Hall Art Gallery, 1979.
Collingwood, P. *The Techniques of Sprang. Plaiting on Stretched Threads.* Faber, 1974.
Grierson, S. *The Colour Cauldron.* Mill Books, Perth, 1986.
Hansen, E. *Tablet Weaving. History, Techniques, Colours, Patterns.* Hovedland, Højbjerg, 1990.
Hoffmann, M. *The Warp-Weighted Loom.* Universitetsforlaget, Oslo, second edition 1974.

Essential reading
Ryder, M. L. *Sheep and Man.* Duckworth, 1985.

For the latest research developments see the six-monthly *Archaeological Textiles Newsletter* (obtainable from: ATN, 30 Prince's Road, Heaton Moor, Stockport SK4 3NQ).
For relevant books on textile topics from Shire Publications see the latest Shire Books catalogue.

Index

Page numbers in italic refer to illustrations